LITERARY EVANGELISM
Beyond the Open Mic

I0440207

THERESA HARVARD JOHNSON
Founder of Voices of Christ Literary Ministries International

Published by Lulu.com

Book Cover Design
Higher Ground Publishing & Consulting
950 Eagles Landing Parkway, Ste 302
Stockbridge, Georgia 30281

ISBN: 978-1-4357-7327-1

Printed in the United States of America.
2010 First Edition

*"As each one has received some spiritual gift, **he should use it to serve others,** like good managers of God's many-sided grace - if someone speaks, let him speak God's words; if someone serves, let him do so out of strength that God supplies; so that in everything God may be glorified through Yeshua the Messiah - to him be glory and power forever and ever. Amen."* -- **1 Peter 4:10**

Table of Contents

From the Author

Literary arts ministers have allowed Babylon, our world system, to define who they are as journalists, poets, spoken word artists, novelists, playwrights, song writers, etc. in the congregation of the Lord for far too long. Our identity was, is and always will rest in the very bosom of our Father and it will reflect the very root system of His Word and vision for mankind. I earnestly pray that this simple truth permeates the hearts of the worshipers of this generation and the generation to come like never before.

Father is constantly and consistently drawing us into himself; but to hear him, we must listen and be still. He's drawing us back into studying the Word like the Bereans mentioned in the book of Acts. He's drawing us back into the refining fire of worship, and revealing the heights and depths of intercession and prayer. Everything we need to know about Father and His will for us is rooted here in these foundational places.

He is continuously restoring our identity, our true selves, in Him. *Psalm 139* tells us that He has written all of our days in a book that is stored in Heaven. It's time, prophetic scribes, to ask Holy Spirit to help us open the book that has been written for us; and to show us day-by-day how to walk all of the thoughts and plans out in our lives that Father has written on those pages. We have been called to restore every gift and the function of the gift that has been perverted and stolen from the sanctuary of our Lord – in the capacity in which we've been sent.

I firmly believe that it is only after learning who we are in Christ and *applying* that foundation to our everyday lives that we can effectively walk upright, operate in our gifts and talents; and fulfill our assignments in the earth – according to Father's **original intent and purposes** for us as individuals and as a corporate body.

Note the underlined phrase above. Those who walk with this ministry will quickly tell you that we use it daily. I firmly believe that if we do not know why a thing was ORIGINALLY created, initiated or established by God that we run the risk of misusing it or abusing either out of ignorance or carelessness. My emphasis in ministry is not based on a person's skill or ability; rather, their hunger and thirst for the Lord.

There is a definite place for skill in the worship arts **(1 Chronicles 15:22; Exodus 31)**; but it is skill infused with the Spirit of the Lord that produces godly excellence – the spirit that Daniel carried in his ministry. It is one's life that allows the anointing to flow through – not skill. The Apostle Paul explains this well in **Philippians 3**. He talks about how everything he learned and valued with his carnal mind meant nothing compared with what he gained in Christ Jesus. There is an imbalance in the operation of the worship arts today! This imbalance comes when souls begin worshipping the things that men value, the gift and/or those presenting the gifts instead of God.

This book, *Literary Evangelism: Beyond the Open Mic*, addresses these issues for the prophetic scribe who believes they've been called to strategic evangelism.

There's no solid, biblical guidance for those in the literary arts or the worship arts in general on this subject. This book isn't a "how to" guide full of steps. Instead, it is practical application concerning the Word of God and Father's will for the use of your life and gifts as a scribe. People of God, we need wisdom and instruction that reaches beyond technique, approach, best practices, community norms, entertainment and the cosmetic aspect of our spiritual gifts. We need the kind of wisdom that will keep our eyes fixed on Jesus and empower us to pursue the will of the Father verses the desires and imaginations of men's hearts.

> *"While the focus here is specifically on prophetic scribes, what is written here can easily be applied to ever area of the worship arts."*

There's a cry across the land, specifically for this generation, to *revisit and fully embrace* Father's original purpose and intent for everything we've been given and to take hold of the narrow road outlined in the life of Jesus Christ. That narrow road is just that – extremely narrow, and does not include these broad stretches of scriptural interpretation that so many are presenting.

This book is about the narrow gate. It exposes and confronts wide gates of error, confusion, selfishness and the deep roots of entertainment that blocks, corrupts and destroys HOLY purpose and destiny.

Matthew 7:13 CJB which says this: *"Enter by the narrow gate; for the gate is wide and the way is easy, that leads to destruction, and those who enter by it are many."*

While the focus here is specifically on prophetic scribes, what is written can easily be applied to every area of the worship arts. Please keep this in mind as you read. So many worshipers are pursuing careers in Christ instead of humility and brokenness. They have unknowingly built dens of thieves in their souls and Christ has come to evict them.

After reading this book, it is my prayer that you will truly be in a place of pursuing the Kingdom of Heaven and allowing all that is predestined for you to be added according the scriptures. Father is aligning a remnant of scribes who have given up their desires to pursue record deals and book contracts; bookings, financial rewards and performances; branding, etc. to obey him -- exclusively. These things must no longer be our hearts pursuit.

For additional teachings on prophetic writing, please check out other books in *The Scribal Anointing Literary*® series available through the Voices of Christ website at www.voicesofchrist.org.

May the peace and blessings of the Lord and the **Matthew 13:52** Scribal Anointing overtake you in this season.

Embracing the Ministry of Immersion,

Theresa Harvard Johnson, Apostle & Founder
Voices of Christ Literary Ministries International

Instructions for Personal Study

As you read *Literary Evangelism: Beyond the Open Mic*, I want to encourage you to pray before beginning. Ask Father to reveal himself to you, opening your eyes and ears to receive revelation, instruction, direction, correction and a clearer understanding of your purpose. Keep a prayer journal and record the things Holy Spirit shares as you read.

In addition, I want to encourage you to read each chapter however tempting it may be to skip ahead or only read certain parts. Each chapter builds upon the other – setting a foundation and bringing you fully into several scriptural truths and fresh revelation. Without the foundation, the weight of the message here could be misinterpreted or lost. I firmly believe that this subject is too important for those assigned to it to miss.

This book is written for personal study. It is an opportunity to dig into your own heart. Sometimes when we read, we can focus on what others are doing when in truth the Lord is speaking to us. The topics discussed are intended to give you a starting point for study. It's up to you to go deeper. I've learned so many things the HARD WAY, partly because I had closed my ears to soundness of doctrine and gave in to what I wanted.

You don't have to walk that path. Learn from the wisdom between these pages. At Holy Spirit's leading, I have simply provided some foundational understanding and addressed some of the major points of literary evangelism that I believe every scribe in pursuit of Father should be aware of in the midst of their ministry.

Finally, I encourage you to take your time. Meditate on what you are learning. God has a plan for you as a prophetic scribe. It is my prayer that the fullness of your ministry unto God comes forth in due season and that you are postured correctly to fulfill purpose. *Come, let us take this journey together!*

Brief History of Literary Evangelism

Yes, literary evangelism has a history. Its roots have been around from the first time Moses came off the Mount with the tablets in His hand until now.

Commonly, you will hear the phrase "literature evangelism." That terminology, in particular, has been synonymous with sharing the message of Jesus Christ through the distribution of bibles, religious books, tracks and pamphlets for centuries. Those traditionally walking in this area of ministry refer to themselves as "Christian Literature Evangelists" or say that they are called to Christian Literature Evangelism. In my opinion, it's a very accurate description.

As I've studied out this ministry, I've come to realize that prophetic scribes are also a type of "literature evangelist." We carry the inspired word of the Lord, even what is creative, to ends of the earth through what we distribute. In many ways, we are the increase of what these forerunners started – whether our methods are traditional or involve electronic or audio distribution of what Father pens through us.

I want to pause here for a minute to give a deeper explanation of literary ministry. Literary ministry is a term that I personally use to describe the administration of *The Scribal Anointing*® – the passion and call to write and release the prophetic and inspired Word of the Lord. The prophetic word, as mentioned here, is the releasing of those things that are given to us directly by the Lord to pen and record. The inspired word refers to those things that we write out of our adoration and love of the Father.

The distribution of literature, as we will discuss more intimately shortly, is only a facet of our overall call to scribal ministry as there are many dimensions and levels as revealed through the scriptures. For further understanding, I encourage you to purchase *The Scribal Anointing*® Training & Demonstration Manual and the student workbook, *The Scribal Companion*.

The term "literary evangelism" not only captures the work of those evangelizing through the distribution of literature, but also the ministry of those who are walking out various literary art forms as an intricate part of their ministry. For example, the playwright writes the play and then interprets what is written dramatically. The screen writer records the screenplay and develops it into a short or full-length film.

It is also imperative that we understand that there are two primary ways in which we preach the Gospel. One is through the spoken word - verbal preaching and teaching. The second is the unspoken word. This is non-verbal preaching and teaching through reading, visual presentation (including demonstrations and art forms), and by Christian lifestyle – becoming a living epistle (2 Corinthians 3:3).

The purpose of evangelism has been and always will have a singular, very foundational focus: *To reach as many people as possible with the Good News of salvation through redemption in Jesus Christ.* Our goal between the pages of this book is to reveal one's scribal role in evangelism, and provide those reading with deeper insight and understanding of the critical importance and weight of evangelistic ministry through the literary arts – beyond entertainment and the stage.

Forerunners to Literary Evangelism

Regardless of one's denominational beliefs, it is impossible to talk about literary ministry without acknowledging the impact and legacy of two key forerunners of the 20th Century. Among the oldest and most widely known forerunners are the founders of "Gideon International," the distributors of the Gideon Bible. For well over a century the legacy of Samuel E. Hill, John H. Nicholson and William J. Knights can still be felt around the world. They were true "literature evangelists" whose focus was extremely simple and practical: *Sowing bibles into the lives of men.* Their foundation scripture, **Mark 4:14 CJB**, says it all: *"The sower sows the message."*

People of God, this early example of literary evangelism may not be glamorous, exciting or even seem like a big deal, but I tell you it is a powerful call to ministry. You see, of all the things we do as literary ministers the most valuable piece of literature will always be the Holy Bible. Even as we examine scribal ministry in Jewish culture, you will quickly learn that the most sacred document in existence is, always has been and always will be the Torah scroll, commonly called the Law of Moses. What's even more amazing is that Jewish scribes, even unto this day, have been diligent in protecting the documents, ensuring that not a single ink-stroke is changed in the history of its existence. As believers, we've also come to know that nothing, even the inspired word of God that many scribes receive today, will ever supersede what has already been written.

A statement on Gideon International's website says that Bibles and New Testaments have been printed in more than 90 languages and more than 1.6 billion have been distributed worldwide. Stats from the website state that 700 million Bibles and New Testaments have been distributed in the last 10 years alone. What is even more amazing, at least to me, are the testimonies posted on the website of people who have been in their hotel rooms, hospital beds, prison cells, etc. who were suicidal or hopeless and received comfort from the words of Jesus in these bibles. Can you imagine the testimonies of Christ that have gone forth just from this simple vision?

Today, we see the distribution of literature practiced globally not only through Gideon International but countless other individuals and organizations. It is a commonly known fact that the Holy Bible is by far the most influential, controversial and most widely published and read book in the world! Multiple web sources state that no one really knows how many copies have been printed, sold or distributed.

15

The Bible Society's attempt to calculate the number printed between 1816 and 1975 produced the figure of 2.4 billion. A survey for the years up to 1992 put it closer to 6 billion in more than 2,000 languages and dialects. Who knows what astronomical number we could be looking at today – especially given the influence of digital technology and the Internet. The Bible has traveled and is traveling to places where men have been hindered in delivering the Gospel personally. This would be an excellent example of the "unspoken word."

Another well known forerunner to literary evangelism is Billy Graham, a man whose life and ministry is synonymous with evangelistic outreach, televangelism and crusades. Over the course of his 60 plus years in ministry, he has penned more than 27 books – many of which have led great movements globally in mobilizing individuals, groups and congregations in taking hold of their greatest calling – that of sharing the Gospel and making disciples.

Graham's ministry also has one focus: *To help people find a personal relationship with God, which, he believes, comes through knowing Christ.* The publication of his books, audio, articles and even his magazine, "Decision," has held true to this singular focus for six decades. We can learn a great deal from the examples set by these relevant forerunners.

"Never lose focus of our purpose here on earth which is to help others come to know salvation through the redemptive power of Jesus Christ."

The most important lesson would be this: "Never lose focus of our purpose here on earth which is to help others come to know salvation through the redemptive power of Jesus Christ."

2 Timothy 4:5 CJB says, *"As for you, always be steady, endure suffering, **do the work of an evangelist,** fulfill your ministry."*

A Closer Look at Evangelism

Let's take a closer look at Father's **original purpose and intent** for evangelism. Only in examining this, can we begin to put literary evangelism in proper perspective. The word "evangelist" is a descriptive term used to describe those who "carried the Good News of the Gospel" to others. For clarity, this "Good News" is the full account of Christ's life, death, burial and resurrection for the deliverance of mankind from sin.

Ephesians 4:11 CJB describes the role of the evangelist this way, *"Furthermore, he gave some people as emissaries (apostles), some as prophets, some as proclaimers of the Good News (evangelists), and some as shepherds (pastors) and teachers."* I added the words in parenthesis here for clarity. The actual meaning of "proclaim" is to announce, declare, promulgate, make known, to make known publicly, to publish and to publish by any means necessary.

In **Acts 20:18-21 CJB** the Apostle Paul apostolically and prophetically describes evangelism this way: *"When they arrived, he said to them, You yourselves know how, from the first day I set foot in the province of Asia, I was with you the whole time, serving the Lord with much humility and with tears, in spite of the tests I had to undergo because of the plots of the unbelieving Jews. You know that I held back nothing that could be helpful to you, and that I taught you both in public and from house to house, declaring with utmost seriousness the same message to Jews and Greeks alike: turn from sin to God; and put your trust in our Lord, Yeshua the Messiah."*

For those who are actively evangelizing, there is an insatiable fire burning inside that desires to see souls come into the knowledge of Jesus Christ. The very heart of evangelism rests here – in the ministry of reconciliation.

At the end of the day, this is the apostolic cry of our Father in Heaven – to see His children return to Him. It is from this perspective that we are being pressed by Father to see evangelism as a necessary and critical part of our vocation. It is our purpose to get the message of the Gospel to as many people as possible before Christ returns. People of God, the seriousness of this call cannot be ignored, undermined or downplayed by those of us who have been given the truth.

There is NO GREATER call than this. Is this not what Jesus did during His time on earth? Is this not what he required of his apostles before ascending back into heaven?

Let's take a closer look at **Acts 20** (previous page), and see what the Apostle Paul was directing us to do. The scriptural elements say that we are to:

- **Seek to walk in humility before Father.** Father resists the proud. One of the first barriers that Heaven comes to break within men is pride. Wherever pride exists in your life, there's an area of resistance against you that comes from Heaven. **(James 4:6)** You see, humility allows the POWER of God to flow through us in a greater measure. When we release our resistance to do it our way or have things our way, then the Lord can use us at a much greater capacity. Paul understands what it means to be broken. You see, there are conditions to being effective in ministry. All it takes is a willing heart! **Matthew 18:3-4 CJB** says, *"Truly, I say to you, unless you turn and become like children, you will never enter the kingdom of heaven. Whoever humbles himself like this child, he is the greatest in the kingdom of heaven."*

- **Mourn over sin, injustice and unrighteousness.** The Apostle Paul learned to hate what Father hates and to love what He loves. People of God, our Father hates evil **(Proverbs 6:16-19).** He does not desire to see any man perish under the weight of sin. It is the Father's passion to see His children saved from destruction that caused Him to send Jesus to deliver us. Our relationship with Father should be so intimate that we can experience His heart concerning the sin state of His people. When we see sin, it should cause us to cry out to God for the souls of His people like the prophets and shepherds of old! **Psalm 119:136 CJB** says, *"My eyes shed streams of tears, because men do not keep thy law."*

- **Persevere and press through tests.** In other words, we must get to a place in our walk with the Lord that we are not moved when trials come our way – even from within the Body. Whatever the obstacle, we must learn to obey Father in all things and keep our focus on what we have been sent to do! The scripture that comes to mind here is this: *"Resist the devil and he will flee."* There are, however, lists of conditions that come before that phrase that cannot be overlooked. Read **James 4:2-12 CJB**.

- **Hold back <u>nothing</u> that could be helpful to the Body.** As believers, we must adhere to teaching the truth of God's word to everyone. This means that we are, like Father, to have no respecter of person. Reproof and correction is just as important as encouragement. **2 Timothy 4 CJB** puts it this way, *"I solemnly charge you before God and the Messiah Yeshua, who will judge the living and the dead when he appears and establishes his Kingdom: <u>proclaim the Word! Be on hand with it whether the time seems right or not. Convict, censure and exhort with unfailing patience and with teaching.</u> For the time is coming when people will not have patience for sound teaching, but will cater to their passions and gather around themselves teachers who say whatever their ears itch to hear. Yes, they will stop listening to the truth, but will turn aside to follow myths. But you, remain steady in every situation, endure suffering, <u>__DO THE WORK THE PROCLAIMER of the Good News should,__</u> and do everything your service to God requires."* Take note of the reference to evangelism here.

- **Teach publicly.** One of the things Father has shown me along this journey is that I have an opportunity to share the Good News everywhere I go. If you're truly sold out for the Kingdom and are seeking an opportunity to share, He will present that opportunity to you whether it's with the neighbors in your community or in the check-out line at the grocery store. We must understand that we have a helper – Holy Spirit – on the inside of us who will guide us into all truth. Your only requirement here is to have a willing heart. **1 Corinthians 6:9** says, *"... <u>__for a wide door__ _for effective service has opened to me,_</u> and there are many adversaries."*

- **Teach privately, from house to house.** Never neglect the opportunities that come forth for you to share the Gospel of Jesus Christ privately as well. Unfortunately, we live in a world in which people profusely request payment to bring forth their reasonable service. This practice, no matter how men try to make it appealing, is completely unbiblical. You see, true ministry is focused on snatching souls from hell – not dollar amounts and crowd sizes. If the Lord is indeed calling you to go and proclaim, then you must go! Provision will be made for you within reason. God does take care of His children! We are to enter into evangelistic ministry with the understanding rooted in the word, not in the ideas of men. We should also not neglect the word "privately" either. Small gatherings and one-on-one encounters ARE OKAY. While Jesus did draw multitudes, He also ministered to people one-on-one or within small groups.

- **Be serious about the message of the Messiah and His ministry.** Never take lightly the ministry entrusted to you. Jesus didn't take His ministry lightly or causally. He gave his LIFE – spiritually and naturally. The work that we are continuing is the work that He began. He is not an example of Christian living, but THE example of Christian living. Two scriptures come to mind as I consider this. The first is **Romans 1:16 CJB** which says, *"For I am not ashamed of the Good News, since it is God's powerful means of bringing salvation to everyone who keeps on trusting, to the Jew especially, but equally to the Gentile."* The second is **Revelations 12:11 CJB** which says, *"They defeated him because of the Lamb's blood and because of the message of their witness. Even when facing death they did not cling to life."*

- **Declare the message of repentance from sin to everyone.** The call to repentance is at the very foundation of our evangelistic ministry and can never be lost in the midst of our witness. Never. Above all, we must uphold, protect and represent the philosophy and ideology of our Lord and Savior Jesus Christ in full. Our witness must never fold under the pressure of a people pleasing mentality – the cost is too high. Failing to teach repentance enters one into a ministry of deep rooted compromise. Truly, the Kingdom of Heaven is at hand. You will hear me say this more than once: A message of salvation without mention of repentance of sin IS NOT a message of salvation. **Matthew 3:2 CJB** says, *"Turn from your sins to God, for the Kingdom of Heaven is near!"* Pray that the spirit of John the Baptist fall upon you.

- **Teach truth to everyone – the unbeliever and the believer.** Father has no respecter of persons. An unsaved king needs Jesus as much as the man on the street. Our propensity to release the Gospel can never be based on gender, social class or group, financial status or any of those things that would intimidate the flesh of men. **Romans 2:11-13 CJB** says, *"For God does not show favoritism. All who have sinned outside the framework of Torah will die outside the framework of Torah; and all who have sinned within the framework of Torah will be judged by Torah. For it is not merely the hearers of Torah whom God considers righteous; rather, it is the doers of* *what Torah says who will be made righteous in God's sight." In Greek bibles, the word "Torah" is translated as "the Word."*

- **Teach that our trust must be in Yeshua (Jesus Christ).** In Greek bibles, the word "trust" has been translated as "faith." In short, we are being told to place all faith in Father – holding Him to the performance of His word. **Hebrews 11:1-6 CJB** sums this up best: *"<u>Trusting is being confident of what we hope for, convinced about things we do not see.</u> It was for this that Scripture attested the merit of the people of old. By trusting, we understand that the universe was created through a spoken word of God, so that what is seen did not come into being out of existing phenomena. By trusting, Hevel offered a greater sacrifice than Kayin; because of this, he was attested as righteous, with God giving him this testimony on the ground of his gifts. Through having trusted, he still continues to speak, even though he is dead. By trusting, Hanokh was taken away from this life without seeing death - He was not to be found, because God took him away - for he has been attested as having been, prior to being taken away, well pleasing to God. **And without trusting, it is impossible to be well pleasing to God, <u>because whoever approaches him must trust that he does exist</u>** and that he becomes a Rewarder to those who seek him out."*

Literary ministers, when you consider evangelism in light of the Apostle Paul's insight, it provides a weight of accountability that is far greater than what many perceive. True, pure evangelism means that you must have an **effective** witness of the Gospel. This most effective witness is LIVING what you teach. It is making every effort, every waking moment an opportunity to perfect your trust! This is why the example of evangelism in **Acts 2:36-38** on the Day of Pentecost was so powerful. It would be a blessing to your soul to dig through the scriptures to see true evangelism at work verses looking at many of the examples we see in the Western church today.

Every believer is called to evangelism in some capacity and will walk in it. The scriptures we've walked through are not just for those walking in the office of evangelist or for some special group of people. They are truly for every believer – as we are all evangelists. The distinction in this area of ministry rests in these questions: How deep is your passion to evangelize and how rooted are you in the call?

You see, for the evangelist, this specific administration of the Gospel is their driving force. For those who are not evangelists, the weight of this office is still heavy but it is walked out according to the portion Father has released to them. We must understand this simple truth: Evangelizing doesn't make you an evangelist anymore than prophesying designates you as a prophet. Father can and does use those who are willing. Our role is to let him prepare us, to be open for his direction and to be ready for His use.

Again, <u>every believer</u> is called to facilitate the ministry of reconciliation according to **2 Corinthians 5:18-21** and to make disciples according to **Matthew 28:18-20 CJB** which says:

"Yeshua came and talked with them. He said, All authority in heaven and on earth has been given to me. Therefore, **go and make** *people from all nations into talmidim (disciples)*, **immersing** <u>**them into the reality**</u> *of the Father, the Son and the Ruach HaKodesh, and teaching them to obey everything that I have commanded you. And remember! I will be with you always, yes, even until the end of the age."*

People of God, this is what we're here for. Let's rise to the occasion of our ministry.

1 Peter 3:15 says, *"...but treat the Messiah as holy, as Lord in your heart's while remaining always ready to give a reasoned answer to anyone who ASKS YOU to explain the hope you have in you - yet with humility and fear..."*

Three Levels of Evangelism Today

Over the years, I've found myself evangelizing to three distinct types or groups of people: (1) The lost and unreached; (2) The churched; and (3) the broken and displaced. By no means am I claiming these areas as categories or trying to expand Father's original intent and purpose for evangelism. However, there is a need to acknowledge that evangelism is not only about sharing the Gospel but taking that "sharing" to the next level and *making* disciples. It is only in the making process that one's salvation can be sure – that place of moving from milk to meat.

Let's take a closer look at these types or groups:

- **The lost and unreached.** The lost are those who have not accepted Jesus Christ as their Lord and savior and are therefore not free of sin. A lost soul could be someone who has heard the message of Christ but never took that message seriously or rejected it altogether. The lost or unreached are also those who, for many reasons, have never heard the Gospel message. As a result, the opportunity to receive the word has not been available to them. **(Acts 8:9-13; ACTS 17:16-34 NKJV)**

- **To the churched.** In the Body of Christ, we have people that are bound and institutionalized by religion or legalism. Their subjection to religious beliefs and doctrines are so rooted within them that they are unable to experience the liberty and freedom of knowing Christ fully. In some instances, they may only be playing church and have never had a true encounter. **(Matthew 23; 1 Corinthians 11:13-19; Acts 19:2; Matthew 23:15)**

- **To the broken and displaced.** In Body of Christ, we have people who have disassociated from their faith due to deep wounding either in their personal lives or in the midst of the Church. As a result, they leave the fellowship of the brethren or shut down and isolate; sometimes returning to past sin due to discouragement, lack of faith and unbelief – questioning the validity of their calling. **(Jeremiah 23:1-2; Matthew 23:15)**

In understanding these groups, Father will use us in different ways to reach them. For example, I was riding the train home from work one evening here in Atlanta. I was sitting next to a woman who was clearly minding her own business and seemed to be in deep thought. I clearly heard Father say to me, "Give her that poem you're carrying in your notebook." That was all he said.

Sweating bullets, I fought with the Lord about handing this stranger a poem I'd scribbled in prayer on notebook paper. Needless to say, I lost the battle and handed the woman the paper. Tears began to flow down her face as she read it. Her words to me were: "Only God could have led you to give this me. He does hear my prayers."

She said thank you, asked me if she could keep the poem and continued to weep. In that moment, the Lord had used this poem as part of this woman's reconciliation process in Him.

On another occasion, I felt this compulsion to take a team of poets to a secular open mic venue here in Atlanta. We spent time in prayer and intercession days before going and allowed Holy Spirit to lead and direct us concerning what poems or songs to share. What God did on that night amazed us and opened us up into a deeper level of understanding evangelism – and our role as literary ministers. Let me explain.

As the poets would share, one or two people would approach us afterward to share similar stories from their lives, ask for clarity on something they heard or to request prayer. This was pretty typical on our outings. However, while sitting there listening to the other poets or spoken word artists the Lord began prophetically speaking to me about them. There was one poet in particular whom I later learned was a homeless college student, that I was drawn to on this night. As she shared her poem, which was indeed powerful, it was laced with the spirit of death – suicide, depression, heaviness and hopelessness.

Her delivery was phenomenal and the crowds in the coffee house stood in applause. Yet, I found myself annoyed that no one saw the deep cry for help that came through and beyond the words released. This young woman was in trouble – emotionally and spiritually. Immediate intervention was needed. As the crowds dissipated, I walked over to her and commended her on her delivery, presentation and command for expression. Without hesitation, the spirit of the Lord prompted me to ask her this question: "What inspired this poem?"

Within minutes, she was sharing the trauma of her life over the past few months and confessing how she had made a decision to give up on everything. The power of God fell over us immediately and I began to tell her about the healing power of Jesus Christ. As I drove home that evening, all I could think about was what would have happened if I had not been obedient to the Lord that night. Would he have sent another or would this young woman be another statistic? I was able to press past my own fear and introduce this young woman to Jesus. The decision to embrace Him was hers, but the opportunity – Glory be to God – did not pass her by.

It was during these times that Father increased my understanding concerning evangelism through the arts. Through prayer and intercession, we began forming evangelistic teams among Father's creative scribes and ministering to people inside and outside of the church on very specific topics from the need for salvation to the exposing of secret sin. Everything we did would conclude with souls being reconciled to Christ.

Scribes of the King, we cannot limit ourselves to how the Lord will use us! Every area of the literary arts will touch one of these groups or types.

Ministry Outside the Box

How Father uses you to evangelize or proclaim the Gospel is as unique to you as you are in your uniqueness in Father. While we share a common passion for the Gospel and are loved equally in the Father, every person has distinct characteristics physically and spiritually that make them different.

Early in my walk with the Lord, I was a member of a Church that formed an evangelistic team. All the leaders in that church were required to join – including me. I would take these classes (which were held weekly) and then be expected to participate in evangelistic ministry with the group on weekends. For some reason, I could never get into the groove using the techniques shown to me. We were required to:

- Meet as a team.
- Go into a subdivisions or apartment complexes.
- Knock on doors.
- Hand out literature – including info about our church.
- Ask if people had a relationship with Jesus Christ.
- Walk the unsaved through this "prayer of salvation"

To be honest, I was *very* uncomfortable with this from the start. I lacked the interest, the enthusiasm, the drive and passion to see it through the way I was being taught. The teachings on evangelism were biblical and there were people who fell right into the groove. No matter how obedient I was or how much I prayed, I couldn't catch the fire for this. As weeks passed, I became increasingly agitated, frustrated and discouraged. I even questioned if I had what it takes to evangelize. It was then that Father began to deeply minister to me. He said plainly, *"Prophet, some of this is me and some of it isn't."*

As I share this testimony, I am in no way condemning or criticizing this church or any other ministry who evangelizes this way. I am simply saying that I, THERESA, received a revelation from God in the midst of this that changed my life. I doubt I would have gained the understanding that I'm about to share had I not had this experience. Father began showing me that the fire of evangelism was indeed within me, but that I needed to *seek Him* concerning how to walk out my INDIVIDUAL purpose and destiny in this area. Only then, he said to me, would I be effective in the corporate body. While my call to ministry was that of a prophet and not an evangelist, I was still called to evangelize as we all are according to our portion. I began having an increase of evangelistic dreams and visions using the PROPHETIC dimension of *The Scribal Anointing*® on my life. Follow me for a moment with this.

In my dreams, I would see choreographed-poems, skits and plays in which people would be drawn into the very presence of God. I would see the saved, the unsaved and the compromising believers coming in by droves to be entertained. Instead, Father would touch the deep recesses of their hearts through the worship released through literary arts and the fire of repentance would break out where we were. In these dreams, complete transformation was taking place in the hearts and minds of God's people. Unbelievers were being drawing into the presence of the Lord for salvation and healing. The lukewarm was receiving conviction and getting a fresh fire from the Lord, and those filled with the Spirit were moving into strategic places of increase through worship, intercession and prayer.

It was then that I realized MY PORTION in evangelism was to walk it out THIS WAY! While Father could very well use me going door-to-door, I would be most effective in this capacity. In the next section, I will talk about this more.

As I write this, I can testify today that the Lord has brought these dreams to pass. The ministry of VOC has walked it out many, many times. We must follow Father's lead concerning HOW we are to administrate our gifting in our ministry. It is good to be obedient to leadership but we must also be obedient to God for the purpose of impact. Walking in the area you are ANOINTED to walk in will bring forth power and a HARVEST. Also, understand that just because Father uses you in one way today doesn't mean this is the ONLY way you are going to be used. I've met many prophetic writers who "get stuck" in being used by God in a certain way; but I tell you, we must remain open to every shift and turn in our ministries. You may be traveling the open mic circuit in your evangelistic ministry today, and tomorrow Father may have you forming street teams in the local park.

Be open to the move of Holy Spirit. Let him mature those tools that have been placed in your hands.

Apostolic-Prophetic Evangelism

We are going to shift gears in this section. It may seem like I've stepped off the grid but bear with me. We are digging deeper into God's original purpose and intent for evangelism. This particular aspect is CRITICAL for the prophetic scribe and other worship artists.

Genesis 1:1-3 CJB says, *"In the beginning God created the heavens and the earth. The earth was unformed and void, darkness was on the face of the deep, and the Spirit of God hovered over the surface of the water. Then God said, "Let there be light"; and there was light."*

The phrase, *"...God created...,"* speaks to the immense creativity that flowed from Father in the BEGINNING. This moment in time captures the entire plan for creation – every thought and idea that He pondered in His heart. It encapsulates all that is, that was and that is to come. In that one phrase, the master of all things sets eternity for mankind in motion. Just take a look at his handy work today – we were hidden inside that short phrase *"....God created."*

It is from this massive place in the MIND OF GOD (that place of vision for all existence) that the celestial realm was formed. It is from this place that the uniqueness of the earth, every creature, land formation, vegetation and human kind came forth.

"In the beginning, God created...."

This place of our beginnings is in actuality, the **"apostolic atmosphere and apostolic Kingdom"** in which Father exists – everything he has predestined flows from this place.

God is the apostolic. This apostolic Kingdom is the absolute highest seat of authority in existence and all creation rests under its mantle. As a people created in His image, we've all received a small measure of His apostolic vision.

We are like the artisan Bezaleel. Father calls us, trains us, anoints us and then sets us apart for a specific work. That "specific work" is the releasing of the APOSTOLIC VISION that he has for our lives – those varying assignments that we were predestined to walk out in the earth.

Read what the scripture says about Him below.

Exodus 31:1-6 CJB says, *"ADONAI said to Moshe (Moses),* **_"I have_** **_singled out_** _B'tzal'el (Bezaleel) the son of Uri the son of Hur, of the tribe of Y'hudah (Judah)._ **_I have filled him with_** _the Spirit of God - with_ **_wisdom, understanding and knowledge concerning_** **_every kind of_** **_artisanry._** **_He is a master of design_** _in gold, silver, bronze, cutting precious stones to be set, woodcarving and every other craft."*

Note that Bezaleel was (1) singled out for a specific work; (2) filled with the Spirit of God; and that (3) he was called a master of design. When the spirit of God "filled him," he also received wisdom, understanding and knowledge in the AREA where he was called to go forth.

We are image bearers of the Father. Clearly, the scriptures tell us this. You and I exist in the very center of this apostolic Kingdom – as partakers of the aspects of the *same* creativity that spoke creation into existence. Let's take this deeper.

Genesis 1:3 says, *"...and the **_Spirit of God_** **_hovered_** **_over the surface_** of the water."*

The "Spirit of God" was waiting, watching, and moving prophetically in the midst of this apostolic atmosphere waiting for apostolic direction from the Lord which was the command to move. This "water" is the life giving Word of God. It represents the prophetic - the awakening of, the activating of, the filling of and the bringing forth of those words/commands spoken by God.

You see, when revisiting **Exodus 31** you can see that Bezaleel was SINGLED OUT by God at a specific time for a specific purpose. You will see that Father had an apostolic vision that needed to come forth in the earth. He FILLED Bezaleel WITH HIS SPIRIT to carry out that apostolic vision. The water of the word began flowing through this master craftsman enabling him to **PROPHETICALLY BRING** that APOSTOLIC VISION from Father into the earth realm. Not only was Bezaleel endowed with a gift to complete the assignment, but he was supernaturally anointed to walk it out according to the instructions given to him.

While we have been given the apostolic vision, our MOVING in that vision is prophetic in every aspect. We are literally allowing Father's spirit to stir within us until we are commanded to move. This makes everything we do, at the command of God a prophetic act! It's not just "doing something." Because of this foundational truth, we must understand that we can't do just anything or move just any kind of way! We are all APOSTOLIC people, moving under a PROPHETIC anointing. This movement isn't limited to "certain" people or just those with "titles." We've got to get this.

This is why it is so imperative that we clearly HEAR GOD and not haphazardly "do ministry." The effects of the wayward are devastating in the realm of the spirit.

I want to encourage you to read the **Exodus 31** in its entirety. Pay close attention to how detailed Father's apostolic vision was for what He wanted to create. Note that the anointing on Bezaleel was given to walk out that specific assignment. I am thankful that He obeyed the Lord in every detail. Can you imagine what His assignment would have resulted in had he chosen to go his own way --- and disregarded the instructions Father had released to him?

People of God, the same thing that was expected of Bezaleel in his gifting and ministry is expected of us today. Father requires this same kind of holiness, sanctification, loyalty and excellence of service. Walking out our assignment is not just about the gift, but following every prayerful detail we've been given. We cannot afford to continue to do ministry out of our minds or good ideas.

I don't mean to be so repetitive, but we have to get this. Father is literally calling us to bring what he released in His apostolic Kingdom into the earth.

> *Our "creativity" is, in truth, a prophetic demonstration of and the walking out of apostolic vision in the earth.*

The key is this: We must understand that God doesn't just give us great poems, skits, books, screen plays and such just to be admired and enjoyed by others. He is actually filling us with apostolic vision and the poems, skits, books, screen plays, etc. are strategies implemented through YOU to bring those vision forth in the earth in the timing He has ordained.

It is from this perspective that we discuss "apostolic-prophetic evangelism."

In the ministry of the arts, we are "moving or being led" as the Spirit of the Lord directs us. **If I had to define apostolic-prophetic evangelism,** I would simply say that it is the ability to "hear and receive strategies from Heaven concerning preaching the gospel and making disciples; and implementing those strategies according to the _exact instructions_ received from the Lord for us as individuals." For the prophetic scribe, our instructions may vary from the releasing of poetry to illustrating the word through skits or plays. Father gave us this creativity and the passion to worship him in this way, and He is the one who will direct how we are to use the gift. No book or acting class can direct what has been orchestrated by Heaven. It may help us develop the skill, but the vision and direction comes only from the Lord.

Also note that Father anointed Bezaleel to choose leaders to assist him.
But even in this, this artisan was given instructions on whom to choose.
Generally, evangelism has been a literal act – one in which we are taught HOW to evangelize verses allowing men to get their specific directives from Father. When your literary arts gift is saturated and rooted in a place of pure worship and intercession they produce power and open the door for the anointing to work through you. Then, when you move into a place of "apostolic prophetic evangelism" it will shift atmospheres, destroy strongholds – especially in the presence of entertainment – **and pull down barriers in the hearts of men that can often prevent them from receiving from the Lord.** Don't forget this. Thus, men's hearts are drawn to the overpowering presence of our God verses the amusement and entertainment of men.

Have you ever heard a ministry song, watched a play or experienced a dance that ministered to you so powerfully that all you could do was cry out to the Lord in repentance, gratitude, thankfulness or an intense reverence? For the unbeliever, this experience could leave them in a place of weeping, brokenness and understanding that Christ is real.

I'm not talking about an emotional response, but a spiritual response that causes godly emotions to come forth as souls are convicted of sin, their hearts are crushed to a point of repentance and they experience the love of God through a personal encounter. If so, you've experienced **apostolic-prophetic evangelism** through the arts – the cry, sound and move of the Kingdom through varying art forms – including literary ministry - that is *strategically* designed to reconcile the souls of men with the will of God.

It is an aspect of evangelism that **clearly separates the minister from the entertainer.** It an area of evangelism that has been grossly misunderstood, abused and overlooked mightily in our congregations and by the worshipers. It is an aspect of evangelism that will quickly reject any mingling or mixing whatsoever with the practices and influences of the world system.

Digging Deeper

Jesus Christ left us with an urgent command in **Matthew 28:18-20.** I firmly believe that this is one of the most important mandates released from God into the earth – and the ultimate act of love. This passage is also at the very core of Father's apostolic vision, which is to fully restore us back to Him. No matter what you teach, how well you perform or how many people speak of your greatness, there is absolutely no vision in Heaven or in earth greater than that of reconciliation.

Father has moved many literary arts ministers into intense evangelism in this hour. I found myself asking the Lord why? He simply said, *"I am not leaving a single stone unturned. The Gospel must be preached by any means necessary."*

In other words, Father is using every gift to achieve this singular purpose. I often tell scribes who are drawn to acting – that they **are not actors** at all. The term acting is for those rooted in this world-system and driven by this world's ideals for performance and fine arts. Whenever I talk about this or other subjects along these lines, it really causes people to become angry.

I've been accused of going overboard in my understanding and being very opinionated. I tell you, when you stand on the true word of God – you will be seen as opinionated, judgmental and critical. But that's okay because the road to holiness and sanctification is NARROW. There's very little wiggling room. Again, all we need to do is read our word to discover this. For some reason, people believe that "they are losing something" when we speak against performance and entertainment.

The truth of the matter is this: If people sought Father's plan for their gifts instead of their intellect and desires, their entire ministries would transform and UNDERSTANDING concerning what I speak of would be made clear. Sometimes my heart cries out before the Lord because I desire to see people DEFEND THE GOSPEL and their belief in Jesus, the way they defend and justify things that will burn up like "performance and entertainment."

We are truly not of this world though we live in it. I pray that a deeper understanding of who we are in Christ comes to each and every soul who picks up this book. We are a SET APART people who live in an apostolic atmosphere that is singularly focused on reconciling mankind to the Lord.

In continuing with this example, the words "actor or actress" indicates that individuals are pretending or performing. The Lord doesn't consider _anything_ scribes do in His name in that light.

The truth is this: Those in the Kingdom who have a passion for this area of ministry, are in fact, _prophetically_ interpreting, demonstrating and illustrating the prophetic word of the Lord.

Let me explain this. As a prophetic writer, I often receive skits from the Lord in dreams or visions. I write down what I believe the Lord is showing me. Most of the time, a theme emerges and I begin to see a clear message come through the skit that represent biblical truths – messages that the Lord would like to get into the hearts of men to awaken them in some way.

Well, it didn't take me long to realize that these creative visions and dreams for skits were really "prophetic words." But instead of receiving them as a prophecy per se, I was seeing them illustrated by people. In truth, these skits were prophetic. When I released them in the way Father directed, they would in fact "prophesy" to the people.

Take a look at key leaders and especially the prophets of the bible who exemplified this.

Did not Jacob rend his cloths and put sackcloth over his loins to demonstrate mourning? Did not Jeremiah wear a yoke around his neck to demonstrate a prophetic word he received from God? Did not Mordecai put on sack-cloth and ashes and walk through the city? Did not John the Immerser eat locusts, wild honey, and wear clothes made of camel's hair? Did not Moses us a staff to demonstrate God's power? Did not Christ speak in very visual parables to reveal biblical truths?

Did not EZEKIEL use all manner of illustration to walk out the prophetic words he received from the Lord? Some of the things he did were down-right strange, but each one was significant in ILLUSTRATING the word of the Lord for His people. _In each instance, there was an unspoken, spoken and creative demonstration or illustration of the word coming forth – prophetically._

We ARE NOT ACTORS but ILLUSTRATORS of a very real prophetic word from the Lord. People of God, we have to ask ourselves a very, very serious question, "Why do we need to identify with the world for our identity? Why is it important for us to be labeled as performers, actors or entertainers?"

Please understand that I know Father will place us in environments and situations to be a light in the midst of darkness. This is clearly understandable. However, we are NOT to take on the appearance of the world. It is our duty to follow the Lord step by step in intercession and prayer to ensure that we do not become a pawn in the very environment we're suppose to over take!

Father has not changed! We may have more stuff than the world did thousands of years ago, but the word of God is still the same. What I want you to grasp here is the POWER that is embedded in YOU when you walk in your **CONSECRATED** gift – lead solely by the Spirit of the Lord verses good ideas and intellect! I want you to value what Father has given you and to begin to see it as more than this neat gift or a way to be entertained, make a name for yourself, get wealth or to entertain others. People of God, your ministries are serious, not frivolous.

Let's go back for a moment.

During my experience on the evangelism team at the church I mentioned earlier, I spent a great deal of time conversing with Father about what He was revealing to me. I tell you, I was so overcome by His love during that time despite the struggle. I didn't want to be a rebellious leader, yet I also knew that I could not continue in the evangelistic role that I was being walked out before me. Eventually, I went to the leadership and shared what I was experiencing and what God had revealed. I acknowledged the strong call inside me to evangelize and embraced the uniqueness in the ministry of my heart. The scripture I'm sharing below began illuminating itself to me like never before! In it, I found confirmation and freedom.

1 Peter 4:10-11 CJB puts it this way: *"As each one has received some spiritual gift, he should use it to serve others, like good managers of God's many-sided grace - if someone speaks, let him speak God's words; if someone serves, let him do so out of strength that God supplies; so that in everything God may be glorified through Yeshua the Messiah - to him be glory and power forever and ever. Amen."*

You see, it confirmed to me that I had to use what Father had placed in me to fulfill my evangelistic call to ministry. Did this mean I would never do door-to-door evangelism again? Did this mean I would never reach out to a soul in a parking lot, a doctor's office, a subdivision, a housing complex or a gas station? Absolutely not! Everywhere I go is an opportunity to share the good news. It simply meant that I was free to **be** who God had created **me** to be AND that I did not have to put evangelism in a tight box that said, *"This is the way you have to do it!"*

34

I'm not sure if the leadership understood my position on this or not, but I was released from that assignment. I walked away knowing that the dreams that I was receiving were actually **apostolic *strategies*** from Heaven that Father would implement through the prophetic ministry entrusted to me. I also learned that the strategies and ministration of evangelism could be as unique to an individual as that individual is in the Kingdom.

Please know that I am not telling those who read this book to become renegades in the midst of their congregations or to rebel against leadership. We must respect authority, have wisdom and wise counsel. Everything must be done decently and in order. This testimony is for your understanding and prayerful inquiry before the Lord.

What I am saying is that we cannot neglect the *specific administration* of our gifts as released by Holy Spirit. There were many areas in the evangelism training I received that were valuable to me. There were also a number of things that were clearly the ideas of men that needed to be discarded. What I love about Holy Spirit is that He is the revealer of truth! He is well able to do any correcting in the earth realm that Father requires.

Even as we fellowship and move within the Body of Christ we must allow Father to guide us in fulfilling our specific call, purpose and destiny. True unity is NOT UNIFORMITY – everyone doing the same thing. It is letting every part of the Body do what it was ordained to do. Our corporate purpose is one that runs like a well oiled engine – every part contributes to the whole. As we dig deeper into this teaching, it is my prayer that you receive all that Father has for you, and that YOU will not leave this earth with your scribal purpose and destiny unfulfilled. I am convinced that every good work that our Lord has begun in you will be completed!

You Are a Specialist

Psalm 139:14-16 CJB says, *"I thank you because I am awesomely made, wonderfully; your works are wonders -I know this very well. My bones were not hidden from you when I was being made in secret, intricately woven in the depths of the earth. Your eyes could see me as an embryo, **but in your book all my days were already written;** my days had been shaped before any of them existed."*

The word specialist has deep meaning for me. Bezaleel was a specialist. King David was a specialist. I pray that after completing this book, the word "specialist" will have a deeper meaning for you as well.

In Hebrew, the word "special" means <u>fitted completely</u>, distinguished by a mark, a wonder, a sign or a miracle. As David quoted these verses from **Psalm 139,** he was reminding himself of just how "special" he was in the sight of God. He even indicates that every single day of his life was written out in detail in GOD'S book. What's even more amazing is that these things were written *before* our souls entered into the earth realm. Father really ministered to me through this, I began imagining him choosing the month, date, year and exact time that I would be born. I realized that HE was in the details of my DNA and that my existence was NO MISTAKE. **I was born for such a time as this.**

Wow! Can you see yourself in this? Your existence, just like mine, was in that place of *"...God created."* We are here because there's something so intricate to the Apostolic Vision of God that we had to be sent from Heaven to earth! Scribes of the King, that is a revelation we should run with to the ends of the earth as we walk in Father's will for us!

The word "special" is at the very root of "<u>special</u>ist." Varying definitions indicate that a specialist is a person **who has been trained** to be an expert at something. It's not a far stretch then, to conclude that every <u>special</u> soul has a <u>special</u> assignment in the earth. Tapping into that assignment is a matter of plugging into the Lord. (Additional reading: **Jeremiah 29:11; Jeremiah 1:1-4; Romans 8:29; Psalm 8:3-4)**

> *We are here because there's something so intricate to the Apostolic Vision of God that we had to come from Heaven to earth!*

As you continue to read, please know that this discussion about "specialists" will come together as we walk through this section. (To get full understanding, you will need to stick with me even when it seems like I've traveled off the path.)

You see, evangelism has *deep roots* in apostolic vision. Evangelism depends on the prophetic for fulfillment. Truthfully, many of us only scratch the surface of what we've been called to do. My role in your life right now is to give you, Father's prophetic scribe, greater insight into your call to "literary evangelism" – a very special area in evangelistic ministry. While you're working the literary assignment, someone else is working visual arts, dance, music, song, etc. Who knows, you may even tap into some of these areas as well.

You, nor I or the Apostle Paul were called to evangelize haphazardly – meaning without understanding or strategic focus. Many of us walk around with a general understanding of what we are doing, but there comes a time when we must mine the field for the specifics. We must begin asking Father those tough questions like, *"Why do I write this way or release the work you've given me like this or like that?"* If we ask Him, He will answer.

You see, every evangelistic effort inspired by Father is a mission from Heaven that results in a harvest – whether you see the harvest manifest or not. If it doesn't result in a harvest – whether seen or unseen – then true evangelism never too place. In the military, when a soldier is deployed he or she is sent on a mission. The completion of that mission is considered a success regardless of whether that soldier actually sees a tangible outcome. When we are sent into the mission field, all we are required to do is follow our orders like any soldier in an army. Everything that we do in the midst of that is an assignment.

There have been times when I've evangelized over an open mic at a secular poetry venue or other events, and soon afterward people would come up to ask for prayer, share personal testimonies, heart wrenching stories or inquire about the piece I shared or the delivery style. Whatever the case, I took the time to listen to them, pray when needed or answer questions as they arose. On many, many occasions these relationships moved beyond simply administering a word of reconciliation and into a place of discipleship and mentoring.

Father began showing me that every piece of prophetic writing is actually assigned to a specific person or group for a specific time in Heaven and in the earth. While we cannot always see the impact, there is a knowing on the inside of us that something powerful has taken place – even if no one ever clapped, shook their keys or came to tell you how great that was when you were done. While that writing I released could be for me, I came to understand that it was also for someone else. When released in the timing of God, just like prophecy, it would produce fruit. Father's word does not return back to Him unfulfilled.

On a side note, there's also a demonic element to this. When we release soulish assignments or when hell's scribes release demonic assignments, bondage ensues. But that's another subject.

I tell you, it didn't take me long to realize that my obedience in evangelizing "in the way" the Lord had given it to me had impact. My evangelistic tool was, in part, poetry and spoken word. I began to see every poem as a hand grenade or a nuke in the realm of the Spirit. Father begin showing me that each Holy

Spirit inspired poem had a soul attached to it. For you, that could be a poem, a spoken word piece, a song, a play or skit, a devotion, etc. Just like those Gideon Bibles that people in jail cells and hospitals encountered; your writing could have the same impact!

When I went forth in ministry at these venues under the covering of pure evangelism as revealed to us by the Apostle Paul, souls received a touch from the Lord. Seeds were being planted and watered in the hearts of the hearers, and God alone was releasing increase.

As I considered these encounters over time, I began realizing that Father was using me specifically in the open mic arena. Before long, it became apparent to me that my poetry often addressed healing from emotional, physical and sexual abuse. Holy Spirit was leading me to address issues of rejection, abandonment, fear and intimidation in a very unique way. It left those listening moved and longing for healing. It left them encouraged to pursue their freedom in these areas in Father. It was also in this place that a light bulb came on inside me and Father begin to reveal that my literary ministry (and call to ministry overall) would be one in which I would be used to help release Father's people from the strongholds of relational and sexual sin – particularly in the area of sexual abuse. The more I wrote and released, the greater the passion for this area of ministry became.

The Lord began drawing those people to me who also had similar passions. Without realizing it, I began teaching and mentoring them as they came at the hand of Holy Spirit. Scribes of the King, Father had moved me from the door of evangelism to active discipleship in 0 to 60 seconds! The "specialist" that He'd prophesied concerning and written about in that book in Heaven was coming forth in the natural. My testimony is sharing this story with many other literary ministers who seeking to find their way. We cannot remain on the banks of the river in our evangelistic call.

I tell you, when we learn to bend into the ways of the Kingdom and block the ways of the world we will see great transformation take place in us and in others; and Kingdom understand will fill our minds as wisdom builds her house in our hearts. Father wants us to walk in our area of specialty. Did not he call forth the most skilled artisans to build the temple and make the priestly garments? You see, there was a special anointing Father was in need of to accomplish those tasks.

Masters in the Midst of Specializing

Take another look at this passage of scripture.

Exodus 29:1-5 CJB says this, *"ADONAI (The Lord) (Moses) said to Moshe, I have singled out B'tzal'el (Bezaleel) the son of Uri the son of Hur, of the tribe of Y'hudah (Judah).* **I have filled him with the Spirit of God - with wisdom, understanding and knowledge concerning every kind of artisanry.** <u>**He is a master**</u> *of design in gold, silver, bronze, 5 cutting precious stones to be set, woodcarving and every other craft."*

Prophetic Scribes! Father wants us to be *masters* of what we are called to do – operating in a spirit of excellence and in excellence of skill as one trained under Holy Spirit.

He is saying to you today that your ministry is integral to the Kingdom! The poem, the acronym, the acrostic, the play, the song, the devotion, the novel or whatever it may be that He has given you has purpose. If you allow Him, He will teach you to be a master and you will do the exploits in His name that you were predestined to do! What has Father called you to be a master of?

Whatever it is will be used for His Glory! Evangelism is only the beginning for those who do not know God or who have strayed away from Him. Evangelism expedites reconciliation in a heart ready to receive. It positions them to be fully discipled and set on a path to maturity.

Let's take a closer look at **Matthew 28:18-20 CJB**: *"Yeshua (Jesus) came and talked with them. He said, "All authority in heaven and on earth has been given to me. Therefore,* **<u>go and make</u>** *people from all nations into talmidim (disciples),* **<u>IMMERSING them into the REALITY</u>** *of the Father, the Son and the Ruach HaKodesh (Holy Spirit),* **<u>and teaching them to obey everything that I have commanded you.</u>** *And remember! I will be with you always, yes, even until the end of the age."*

From the Hebrew perspective, our role in making disciples is one of "IMMERSION" – the drenching of Father's people into the knowledge of who is He is! The Greek word "baptize" doesn't fully capture what is meant to take place in this discipleship process. Broken down, the word "immersion" is interpreted as meaning to be dipped repeatedly; to submerge (of vessels sunk); to cleanse by dipping or submerging, to wash; to make clean with water; to wash one's self; and to overwhelm by bathing. John the Baptist was actually *John the Immerser.*

Today, we are the forerunners who are preparing the way for Christ's return. We will never fill the shoes of John the Immerser, but we can learn to carry that message of repentance that rested in his belly.

John's excellence of spirit in his administration of his call as a prophet, made him a master. He is the only prophet whom Christ referred to as being great. In The Scribal Anointing, we learn that there was only one scribe whom Father referred to as being a scribe instructed in the Kingdom of Heaven. We know that in the area of wisdom – only Solomon coveted the greatness of that honor. When it comes to a triumphant example of pastoralship, we have Moses to look up to.

People of God, MASTERS should be in our midst. We should be able to identify them by excellence of spirit AND excellence of skill in the areas where they are called.

Moving In Your Specialty

We just talked about being "special" and being "specialists" in the Kingdom. We've also covered these simple truths: (1) You have been given the ministry of reconciliation and (2) You have been called to make disciples. From this point forward, settle these truths in your heart, understanding that these things are a part of your reasonable service in the Kingdom.

But even as we go out to proclaim the gospel with this understanding, Father is preparing us to even do that with precision. In an army, you have very specific companies whose soldiers are organized by their strongest skills, abilities and specialties. They are given specific assignments that fit those skill sets. It's the same way in the Kingdom of Heaven. You and I are most effective in the areas where we are called.

In the Kingdom, scribal ministry has many facets. This is detailed in the *The Scribal Anointing*® Training & Demonstration Manual. In addition to being called into a particular type of scribal ministry, you may also walk in one of the **Ephesians 4:11** ministries – that of the Apostle, Prophet, Evangelist, Pastor or Teacher. If that is the case, your scribal ministry, even as you evangelize, will be one that carries the weight of the "office" of a:

- Scribal Apostle
- Scribal Prophet
- Scribal Evangelist
- Scribal Pastor

- Scribal Teacher

In other words, your "scribal ministry" will reflect your function in whatever area you are called to walk in. (In this book, we are not digging into each of these individually; but further information is available online through the Voices of Christ website and through our prophetic school of the scribe.)

We can drill this down even further to reflect your uniqueness in the midst of that ministry call. Our Father is beyond amazing people of God. When we are tapped into him, we walk out our "purpose" in everything that we do.

For example, I am Father's scribal apostle. This is in me just like prophetic demonstration was in Jeremiah and Ezekiel. My functionality in this office brings order to congregations and alignment to leaders concerning pure ministry. When you hear me speak on ANYTHING the discussion of *pure ministry* – becoming a living epistle - will be at the forefront. Everything that I write and teach carries this sound. I can't help myself. If I summed up my passion for ministry in Christ, it would be to see every soul "...IMMERSED in the REALITY of the Father, the Son and Ruach Hakodesh" according to **Matthew 28:18-20**. In truth, it's a passion to see others take their vocation, whatever it may be, seriously.

People of God, you need to know just how special you are in the army of the Lord! You were custom built for your call – from your Holy Spirit shaped personality all the way down to your role in the Kingdom. **You need to be aware of your specialty.**

As you study the patriarchs of the Bible, begin to ask the Lord what they were sent to do in the midst of their call to ministry. Every SOLDIER in the army of the Lord has a specific assignment and weapon, like the literary arts, to help them accomplish each mission that comes their way.

In addition to delivering us, Jesus Christ was sent to give us a perfect example of how to walk this walk before God and men. The Apostle Peter was sent to release to us how to walk in trust and have faith in God – to a point where even our shadows can bring healing and deliverance. The Apostle Paul left us with a legacy of "finishing" the race despite your past and present circumstances. We can never discount ANYTHING that Father has given and truly, what He has given is specific, special and unique to YOU.

Evangelizing Through the Literary Arts

I know we've covered a great deal of information and revelation up to now; however, we really can't move forward without looking at another aspect of our literary call to evangelism and that is: *Who is the Lord calling me to evangelize to in this season?*

Now, I am not asking this question in a legalistic sense. Some people put themselves in boxes saying, "This is how the Lord uses me or I am only used this or that way." I've said this before and I'll say it again, "Don't limit how the Lord will use you OR who He will use you to witness to in this hour." While you may minister at varying open mics and venues using your worship arts gift; he can very well use you in a local congregation, a grocery store parking lot or on the city bus. These things are totally and completely up to the Lord – not you. Just be ready!

You do, however, need to seek understanding concerning the "sound" inside you or the "voice" you have for the things the Lord. This sound or voice can be defined as:

> "…the message the Lord placed on the inside of you that fuels your passion for ministry."

The voice that is inside me can be summed up this way: "Jesus Christ did not come to entertain you, but to set the captives free." Everything that I teach, say and do comes back to this very simple truth concerning my passion for the Gospel of Jesus Christ. In addition, this message also comes out of me in a very "preachy" manner so-to-speak. I don't agree with the negative connotation of this description, but "preachy" is the only word that I can think of to adequately describe the teachings, books, poetry and spoken word that is often released to me from the Lord.

I've come to understand that my heart for the Lord is very much like that of John the Immerser. Now, I am not claiming to be like him per se; but I am saying that I am one who desires everyone I come in contact with to ENCOUNTER GOD and be transformed. John the Immerser truly set an excellent example for evangelism.

Identifying Your Sound

You must take the time to identify your sound.

Your sound is not the rhyme in your poetry or spoken word. It's not the "beat" in the midst of your rap or even the swag (some form of charisma) that you bring into a room when you show up. They play a role in your life but they do not "identify" *your sound*.

When considering the definition in the previous section, biblical examples may look like this:

- **Moses' sound:** "Let my people go. It's time to come up out of Egypt."

- **Abraham's sound:** "There's a new land ahead that Father desires to bring us into it. Let's go there, do all that is required, build, prosper and multiply in His name."

- **King David's sound:** "In everything, pursue Father's presence and worship him."

- **Prophetess Deborah's sound:** "There is victory in the midst of every battle and God's judgment is just."

- **Prophetess Anna's sound:** "I will pray and intercede until I see the promise of the Lord."

- **The Apostle John's sound:** "Learn to lay your head on Christ's bosom, trust him in all things as you go out to proclaim the good news."

- **The Apostle Paul's sound:** "Nothing learned in this life can amount to what you gain in Christ."

- **John the Immerser's sound:** "Repent, for the Kingdom of Heaven is at hand."

- **Onesimus' sound:** Father uses the foolish things to confound the wise.

- **Christ's sound:** "I was ransomed for your sin that you might have life and have it more abundantly."

Scribes of the King, your sound will directly reflect your call to ministry. It will bring forth those things that you are to impart from that place of apostolic vision into the earth. These are just examples of the sounds I heard coming from the hearts of some of the patriarchs, servants and matriarchs in the scriptures. These sounds flowed through every aspect of their ministries – whether creative or none creative.

If you really want to tap into your sound, then tap into Father's heart for who you are. All this other stuff doesn't really matter. When we focus all of our attention on growing in maturity and relationship in our journey – these other things have a way of working themselves out. In other words, your obedience to God lines you up with destiny and purpose. You begin to literally learn how to allow the Lord to do the work for you, instead of doing so much out of your own strength.

Literary ministers have been so influenced by Baal in this hour that it has become very difficult to discern what is of God and what is of the world. Many scribes of the King are thinking that a music "style" or a particular poetic delivery style is their sound.

The adversary is cunning. He wants to draw you into a place of scrutinizing "how you *deliver* your ministry" and block you from focusing on the "message you are called to deliver." But in the Kingdom of Heaven, Father fine tunes the message in you and it gives birth to its prophetic delivery in the earth.

Why Your Sound Matters

Why is this relevant to scribal ministry?

It is relevant because your "sound" helps bring understanding concerning <u>who you are called to reach</u> while on assignment in the earth. I challenge you to select one of your favorite biblical patriarchs, servants or matriarchs and then see who their sound was intended to reach. Choose from people in the old and new covenant. For example, Moses' sound was an evangelistic call to the church and Paul's sound was an evangelistic call to the lost and unreached; as well as to the broken and displaced.

At this juncture in my walk with the Lord, my sound is primarily to the broken and displaced; and to the churched -- specifically *leaders* in the body of Christ. It is a resuscitating and aligning sound. It is a sound of correction, preparation and warning. It comes through the prophetic poetry I write as well as visions for plays and skits, and words of instruction. You need to know who you are being used to reach in this season. Again, don't get locked into this! Next week, the Spirit can shift your focus. Then again, this could very well be your mantle for lifelong ministry like it was for some of the patriarchs. People of God, don't allow yourself to get stuck in labeling yourself in the midst of this discovery.

Armed with this revelation, I would never take a poem that I have written that brings strong correction and rebuke to leaders in the congregation of the Lord to "the lost and unreached." Why? They are not able to understand what the Father is saying in this regard. This type of message is not for them. The primary goal of evangelism to a none-believer (the lost and unreached) is to bring them into the knowledge of Jesus Christ.

In this type of environment, Holy Spirit will lead the minister to share testimonies; truth about who Christ is and what he came to do, or otherwise shed light on the need for those present to repent of sin and embrace salvation.

Please understand this: Secular venues are not the arenas to share poetry that exposes problems among the congregation of the Lord or to bring rebuke or correction to God's leaders. Why? Well, an unbeliever (the natural man) is unable to comprehend the things of the spirit. **(1 Corinthians 2:14)**

Releasing plays, sharing testimonies or releasing poetry that rebukes or confronts the church in a secular setting will seem more like an attack in environments before people who hate or have negative preconceived notions about our belief system, and can turn a non-believer even further away from Christ.

I learned this the hard way.

Some years ago, I went to an open mic and did a spoken word piece entitled, *"My People Repent."* In that piece, I addressed the sin in the church along the same lines as prophets of old like Ezekiel, Jeremiah, Amos and others did. The only problem was that I forgot that when the prophets spoke these words of warning and judgment, they did so before the rebellious leaders who were in the midst of facing the wrath of God. As a result of this release, I stepped from the stage amid people who loved the poem because of its flow, style and "the message" – but it began a conversation concerning "Why I don't believe in God" and "Why I don't go to church." I was extremely convicted.

I realized that my motive in sharing that poem was to "show off" my flow and to win the praise of people. If I had done this in a "church centered" environment at the leading of Holy Spirit, it would have brought conviction and agreement in the realm of the Spirit. It would have opened the door for conversation concerning our need for healing as a people.

I have never forgotten the conviction I felt that evening nor how Father ministered to me in the midst of my godly sorrow. It was there that I learned that prophetic poetry has to be released solely by inspiration of the Spirit. From this point forward, I began seeking the Lord through intercession concerning what I should share, when to share it and to whom.

People of God, we do not want to be an offense to the Church or a stumbling block to those in need of Jesus. Yet, so many are walking in this place now.

With this in mind, playwrights and novelists should take a closer look at the skits and novels they write. They should seek God concerning the souls assigned to them and place a prayer covering over these works. I am convinced that certain topics and issues are solely to awaken or ignite those sitting behind the pews; and that others are solely for the lost.

Remember, we are STILL talking about the power of apostolic-prophetic evangelism. Even as a creative people, we cannot move in literary arts ministry VOID of strategic direction and instruction.

Father is well able to identify those assigned to you in this area of ministry. Please, ask yourselves this question: *Is my writing evangelistic, meaning focusing on bringing others into the reality of Christ, or is it geared more toward maturing the body?* Allow Holy Spirit to reveal the answer to you, even if you have to do it novel-by-novel, poem-by-poem or play-by-play. In this next section, the points made here will become even clearer.

Know your sound! Get understanding concerning what that sound has been ordained to accomplish for the Kingdom.

Counterfeit Evangelism

Just as there is true evangelism there is also a counterfeit. The counterfeit is becoming increasingly difficult to identify as leaders and congregations invite the world system into their lives and behind their pulpits. This mixture, when supported by leadership, gives the illusion of certain things "being acceptable" or "okay" before God to those looking in and looking on. When in fact, those things are indeed evil. Sadly, these mixed-up ministers and leaders are leading their congregations and those watching their lives into the belly of misguided belief, compromise and increasing sin – erasing the plumbline that Father has clearly drawn. Christian communities, segments and groups fall in, unknowingly drawn by their own lusts, and incorporate these same wayward examples into their ministries. It's a terrible thing to believe you're doing the work of the Lord, when in fact service is in the kingdom of darkness.

Jeremiah 23:1-2 CJB says this, *"Woe to the shepherds who destroy and scatter the sheep of my pasture!" says the LORD. 2 Therefore thus says the LORD, the God of Israel, concerning the shepherds who care for my people: "You have scattered my flock, and have driven them away, and you have not attended to them. Behold, I will attend to you for your evil doings, says the LORD."*

This is the sleep state that a number of leaders and congregations are in today. Quite frankly, many do not want to hear messages like this from ministers like me. It is so perverted now that when you hear this kind of teaching, people are quick to label that leader as judgmental and too holy; when in fact, the entire bible, in its presentation, is solidly offensive to anyone who willfully practices sin. *(Yep, I said it before.)*

These wayward leaders have actually become "sheep destroyers and scatters." I tell you the truth, false peace is always a clear sign of eminent danger. The enemy rarely enters by obvious means. He seeks out the crack – that unguarded and least obvious place. He's COUNTING on us not noticing his presence.

The adversary's greatest strategy is deception! He thrives off making evil good and good evil. Then before you know it, we're standing like Adam in the garden dealing with the fall-out from Satan's strategic wheat sifting process. We need discernment!

Isaiah 5:20 CJB says: *"__Woe to those who call evil good and good evil,__ who change darkness into light and light into darkness, who change bitter into sweet and sweet into bitter!"*

Counterfeit evangelism has the appearance of or act of evangelism, but it is really a false testimony or a false witness of Jesus Christ. A true witness provides ALL OF THE FACTS and hit the most critical points. A false witness leaves out or dismisses the most critical points.

2 John 1:7-11 CJB says this, *"For many deceivers have gone out into the world, people who do not acknowledge Yeshua the Messiah's coming as a human being. Such a person is a deceiver and an anti-Messiah.* **Watch yourselves, __so that you won't lose what you have worked for,__ but will receive your full reward.**

__Everyone who goes ahead and does not remain true to what the Messiah has taught does not have God.__ *Those who remain true to his teaching have both the Father and the Son.* **__If someone comes to you and does not bring this teaching, don't welcome him into your home.__** *Don't even say, "Shalom!" to him; for the person who says, Shalom! to him shares in his evil deeds."*

Look at those warnings! The Apostle John is laying down a hard word here. He is saying that many have gone out "evangelizing" but DID NOT ACKNOWLEDGE Jesus coming as a man to deliver us from our sins. How many people do you know who won't acknowledge Jesus – all they do is mention God. This gives new meaning to the significance of praying in Jesus Name or acknowledging Christ wherever we go.

Then, look at what he says next: Watch yourself!

This is an apostolic warning. You see, if you don't back away from false teachings like this, you will be drawn in and deceived as we discussed earlier in this chapter. If someone does not bring THIS TEACHING – the one that explains who Christ is and why we must believe in Him – get away from them! We've got to get back to proclaiming the truth of the Gospel as a people!

Take a look at these two charts: **True Evangelism and False Evangelism** on the next page.

True Evangelism

Releases the message of Christ according to examples set in the Word of God. (Matthew 28:18-20; 2 Timothy 4) It always includes practical teaching, preaching and living by example before others. (Uncompromising preaching and teaching of foundational biblical truths are evident).

Teaches the Gospel without compromise. (Hebrews 10:26) This includes (1) clearly defining, acknowledging and identifying sin; (2) clearly defining and acknowledging the consequences of sin; (3) clearly acknowledging the need for repentance; (4) clearly acknowledging the need to accept forgiveness through Jesus Christ and abstain from sin.

Teaches about the consequences of sin.

Teaches mercy and grace with a full understanding of the need for a lifestyle of holiness and sanctification. As a result, they come to understand that their lives are lived in wanting to please God by remaining free of sin.

Declares the message of repentance to everyone. Clearly understands that the message of the gospel is for all people – not just select groups.

Takes the Gospel seriously. The understanding is there that evangelism can take place anytime, anywhere and at every opportunity because time is short and Christ is returning soon.

Explains the value and purpose of fellowship.

Teaches a balanced message about the love of Jesus – one that clearly shows his hatred for sin and response to it; and his compassion and love for righteousness.

Teaches that salvation must be maintained through a conscious effort to remain in Christ.

Teaches that there is only one way to be saved, and that is through Jesus Christ.

False (or Counterfeit) Evangelism

Please note that this is not a complete list and that the items listed are in brief, and have not been fully explained.

Attempts to sell the message of Christ through persuasion, hype, gimmicks & pomp-and-circumstance much like that of a salesman trying to close a deal. Many promises are made and expectations are released. (Carnival acts and shows are often held to entice or draw others to the faith.)

Teaches the Gospel in compromise, releasing partial or incomplete truths. Will not address or fully address sin or the sin-state of man. Presents Christ as a loving God who will accept you into His Kingdom even in your unrepentant sin-state.

Teaches that all you have to do is believe. This is only a part of the Gospel.

Teaches mercy and grace without an understanding of holiness and sanctification. As a result, some may come to believe that once they are saved, they are always saved and cannot be judged to hell when they sin.

Only declares the message of repentance when it is convenient or permissible by men.

Does not take the Gospel seriously. In fact, there is a very casual, loose approach to the Gospel that indicates there is time to waste. The releasing of the Gospel is often lined with political correctness, personal opinions and emotion. It is often event-based and event-driven.

Focuses on recruiting others into a particular denomination, church, group or activity.

Teaches an unbalanced message about the love of Jesus – one that only speaks to his compassion.

Teaches that once you are saved, you are always saved.

Teaches that there is more than one way to be saved.

In the literary arts, we must pay close attention to what we say and how we present the Gospel. It is NECESSARY that the words we release and the demonstration of that word is REFLECTIVE of the Gospel. Otherwise, we are presenting a false Christ or releasing an anti-Christ spirit. Not only must we HEAR GOD, but we must follow His instructions precisely.

Our lives must be rooted and grounded in *prayer and intercession* if we are truly taking our calls to ministry seriously. As the apostle over Voices of Christ Literary Ministries International, I meet scribes weekly who treat their literary projects and ministries like business deals and toys. They take orders at the door and their gifts are merely toys to them. It's heart breaking anytime you see this type of behavior among brethren. Truly, it is abominable before God.

Jesus clearly tells us that if we love Him, we **WILL FEED** His sheep. This feeding is selfless. **Matthew 25:35-40 CJB** says this: *For I was hungry **and you gave me food,** I was thirsty **and you gave me something to drink,** I was a stranger **and you made me your guest,** I needed clothes **and you provided them,** I was sick **and you took care of me,** I was in prison **and you visited me.** Then the people who have done what God wants will reply, `Lord, when did we see you hungry and feed you, or thirsty and give you something to drink? When did we see you a stranger and make you our guest, or needing clothes and provide them? When did we see you sick or in prison, and visit you?' The King will say to them, `Yes! I tell you that whenever you did these things for one of the least important of these brothers of mine, you did them for me!'*

GIVING is an amazing revealing of God's love. I'm not talking about the kind of giving that comes with branding and marketing; but the selfless act of sacrifice, compassion and service as described in **Matthew 25**. Truthfully, many literary artists have fallen into a place of worshiping their gifts and worshiping what that gift creates in the natural before men! They are not rightly identifying the secret lusts and motives of their own hearts – and therefore get sucked in to entertainment. My God! There is DANGER AHEAD!

Danger Ahead: The Rise of Sons of Hell

From what we've discussed so far, it is easy to see that the purpose of the worship arts extends beyond simply moving in the gift. It is true that the gifts exist to glorify the Lord, but he receives the greatest Glory when the weight of what is displayed becomes light to men; therefore turning their hearts toward Him. A key purpose of ministry through the arts is to usher in an atmosphere for healing and deliverance – breaking down walls so that men are drawn into the presence of Father.

When true worship comes forth for the craftsman or artisan, it TERRIFIES the enemy and scatters him according to the prophet Zechariah. The Hebrew word for terrify is "chathath." Several key meanings include to break into pieces, to break down or abolish. In everything we do, the elements of **Isaiah 61** are to come forth in way that reflects Father's apostolic vision.

If you're an encourager, then you're destroying the spirit of heaviness. If you're warning the church about entertainment and exposing secret sin, then you're breaking the strongholds of idolatry and witchcraft. If you're writing about the love of God, then you're crushing hardened hearts and pouring out the compassion of Christ. Whatever you do that is of God, does damage in the camp of the enemy.

Remember that as worshipers, we should be *shifting* **atmospheres** under an apostolic-prophetic mantle. Anything else is purely amusement and entertainment! Evangelism that is not rooted in kingdom purposes is destined to have catastrophic results in the realm of the spirit.

THERE IS DANGER AHEAD: When counterfeit or false evangelism is at work, it gives birth to confusion and perversion. A person "won" into the Kingdom this way can be contaminated and corrupted to a point where they offer no real value to the Kingdom.

This is a dangerous place to be for the "evangelist" as well as the "new convert." Check this out:

Matthew 23:13-15 NAS says this best: ***"But woe to you, scribes** and Pharisees, **hypocrites,** because you shut off the kingdom of heaven from people; for you do not enter in yourselves, **nor do you allow those who are entering to go in.*** [*"Woe to you, scribes and Pharisees, hypocrites, because you devour widows' houses, and for a pretense you make long prayers ; therefore you will receive greater condemnation.]*

Woe to you, scribes** **and Pharisees, hypocrites, because you travel** **around on sea and land to make one proselyte (new believer);** and **when** **he becomes one,** you make him **twice as much a son of hell as** **yourselves."

What Jesus shared here is powerful. Here you have compromising believers heading out to evangelize in their own strength. They are doing what they want to do verses what they've been taught to do. These hypocrites and Pharisees are bound by religious doctrine and are legalistic in their thinking and teaching.

This word of "WOE" is not a good word rolling off Jesus' lips. This word woe indicates great judgment, affliction and misery is on the way. It's like saying, "What have you done you hypocrites! Do you not know the consequences of your false religion!"

My God! In their blindness and rebellion, these men were teaching error and walking in great compromise. They were using their "status" as leaders in the church for personal gain and Christ new it! They had hidden agendas – and were not releasing the whole truth (either by living it or teaching it). Therefore, they were shutting off heaven from those who desperately needed the word of God.

Scribes of the King, YOUR WRITING and your literary ministry should flow from the river of God. It should never be presented in such away that produces compromise and closes the door to salvation in the face of others! I visited a Christian website once that had what appeared to be truth posted in the teachings, but they also preached an aspect of the Gospel that excluded people of color and taught against women in ministry. This is one of many examples concerning how people can "shut heaven" by making the Gospel seem like an "exclusive" club.

In other words, not only are the false teachers (Matthew 7:15) blocked from the Kingdom of Heaven; but those they raise up and who follow their authority can be blocked. This is a frightening place to be!

Then, the scripture talks about how these same false leaders travel all over the world to "evangelize" (counterfeit evangelism) – seeking to win souls; only to win them and then transform them into wicked, misled versions of themselves. We must understand that our corrupt lives will SPILL OVER into the lives of those we lead, influence or otherwise have some charge in discipling.

There are people we see everyday who are the products of "Pharisees and hypocrites." Their leaders have literally cloned them into little compromising and corrupt versions of themselves.

Jesus was very specific here!
Instead of making disciples, these people are raising up **"sons of hell"** who are twice as bad as they are. Wow! I tell you, I wish I could give some

testimonies about the traps I have almost fallen into with this. Truly, I have seen this happen in ministry up close! The offspring of these hypocrites is vicious; and the fallout can only be dealt with at the hand of the Lord.

I thank God daily for awakening, freedom and separation. Truly, I or many of you reading this book could have fallen into this category as a "son of hell" – a child of the adversary.

Don't be found in this condition before God! Don't be among those who believe they are a part of Christ's Kingdom but He doesn't know them. Oh how terrible it would be to do all of this in Jesus name, only to have it mean nothing on the Day of Judgment! **If ever there was a deception that we needed to be aware of, saints, this is it!**

It is one thing to be a hypocrite, but quite another to take others down that path with you. **Jeremiah 23** really explains God's hatred for false teachers or those who bear a FALSE witness of His Son, Jesus Christ. God calls them "scatterers of the sheep." Jesus calls them "hypocrites."

Don't be a **son of hell.** Remember the NARROW gate.

For some, this warning is bit over the top; but for those who hear God I pray that you let it sink in. Surely, this is a reality among believers today as we war to keep Jezebel out of the Tabernacle of the Lord.

John 8:42-45 CJB says, *"Yeshua replied to them, "If God were your Father, you would love me; because I came out from God; and now I have arrived here. I did not come on my own; he sent me.*

Why don't you understand what I'm saying? Because you can't bear to listen to my message. <u>*You belong to your father, Satan, and you want to carry out your father's desires.*</u> *From the start he was a murderer, and he has never stood by the truth, because there is no truth in him.*

When he tells a lie, he is speaking in character; because he is a liar -- indeed, the inventor of the lie! But as for me, because I tell the truth you don't believe me."

The Wide Gate

Matthew 7:13-14 CJB says, *"Go in through the narrow gate; for the gate that leads to destruction is wide and the road broad, and many travel it; but it is a narrow gate and a hard road that leads to life, and only a few find it."*

Briefly, I want to talk about the "narrow gate." For the purposes of this teaching, it can be defined as choosing to make every effort to follow the path Jesus Christ has set for us. It is a place of holding on to the foundational principles we were taught. I tell you, every believer should familiarize themselves with the Sermon on the Mount beginning in **Matthew 5** – asking Father to pour these words over us like fire. These passages speak fully of the narrow way and show us how to clearly govern our lives. This is the only path that leads to Christ Jesus. My heart goes out for the souls of those who would dare believe there is another way.

In contrast, the wide gate is a place of endless opportunities – multiple ideas and options. Not every opportunity, no matter how pleasing and innocent it may seem, is an open door created by God. Many times it is a distraction. One thing can be sure though, it is filled with things we desire, wish for, enjoy doing or that brings us pleasure in the beginning. The doors that open through the wide gate feed our secret inhibitions and desires; and fuels the human soul for earth bound encounters.

Taking the narrow gate is a walk of death to the flesh – as we deny the pleasures of this world for the pleasure of oneness with Christ, our Lord and Savior. We are exchanging temporal happiness for an eternal joy that, in truth, will never measure up to what the wide gate presents.

It's decision time.

Beyond the Open Mic

The purpose of this book is not to condemn anyone, but to bring conviction of sin, urge repentance and realign scribes of the King with their evangelistic purpose. There are many people who earnestly believe that what they are doing in their ministries is "evangelistic in nature" and of the will of God.

They must be awakened to truth.

> *Moving "beyond" the open mic is saying, "Father, I don't need the lime-light, the stage or the acceptance of men to be who you have called me to be."*

Moving beyond the open mic is about completely *immersing* oneself into the apostolic-prophetic vision of reconciliation that is at the forefront of Father's heart and mind. It's going back to our foundational root-system – that place in which the pursuit of holiness, sanctification and righteousness through Jesus is our central focus. Moving "beyond" the open mic is saying, "Father, I don't need the lime-light, the stage or the acceptance of men to be who you have called me to be."

It is where the entire focus of ministry is being vessels that carry forth a "true anointing" as released **Isaiah 61:1-3 CJB** says:

*"The Spirit of Adonai ELOHIM is upon me, **because ADONAI has anointed me to announce good news to the poor. He has sent me** to heal the brokenhearted; to proclaim freedom to the captives, to let out into light those bound in the dark; to proclaim the year of the favor of ADONAI and the day of vengeance of our God; to comfort all who mourn, yes, provide for those in Tziyon who mourn, giving them garlands instead of ashes, the oil of gladness instead of mourning, a cloak of praise instead of a heavy spirit, so that they will be called oaks of righteousness planted by ADONAI, in which he takes pride."*

People of God, the anointing is not your talent or even the mastery of your gift. We've got to get this! So many people speak of the "anointing" and being "anointed." In truth, the anointing only falls on those who earnestly carry the Good News. So many mistake charisma and training in a particular gifting as the "anointing." This couldn't be further from the truth. Moses, Abraham, Isaac, Jacob, etc. were anointed. Peter, James, John, Stephen, etc. were anointed. Why? Because they walked in the will of the Father concerning the assignment entrusted to them. They walked with the Lord, the Lord walked in power with them.

The anointing does not come to tickle emotions or get us in the MOOD for ministry. The anointing is ASSIGNED to heal the broken hearted; proclaim freedom to the captives; release those in darkness into the light; to proclaim the year of the Lord and the day of vengeance of Jesus; to comfort those who mourn; to give beauty for ashes; to give the oil of joy for heaviness; and to give the cloak of praise for heaviness. That's it people of God! When the anointing is truly present – these things will take place. People will not only leave changed, but they WILL REMAIN changed. From this point forward, remember that when you claim the anointing – you are saying that these things are made manifest through you. You are saying that you are walking in miracles, signs and wonders like Christ. He IS the ANOINTED ONE!

When we walk in pure ministry, Father promises to be with us. **This "being with us" is His presence.** It is the presence of the Lord INSIDE us that brings the "anointing" – *not us or the gifts*. When we get this and it truly becomes our desire to see others taste and see the goodness of the Lord, there is nothing Father will withhold from us to carry forth His purpose. Examine yourself! Don't allow men to replace your ANOINTING with people-appeal – charisma!

Exodus 33:15 CJB says, *"Moshe (Moses) replied, "If your presence doesn't go with us, don't make us go on from here."*

While our circumstances may not always be the same as those Moses faced, we must get to a point when we can shout this statement from the rooftop and believe it. Moses wanted to be sure that HIS SOUL and the SOULS FOLLOWING HIM were right with God before going forth. He understood the consequences of walking in ministry WITHOUT the protection or covering of God. In other words, Moses knew they were powerless and unable to do anything in their own strength. He knew that if Father's presence wasn't with him that he'd be walking outside of His will. That's a powerful revelation.

If you take nothing else from what has been shared, meditate on the revelation in **Acts 20:18-21** and **Matthew 28:18-20**.

Moving beyond the open mic is taking a position of humility. Allow Holy Spirit to reveal any area of sin in your life – even that of walking in false evangelism and being guilty of raising sons of hell.

The next step is repentance – the turning away from sin and doing whatever it takes to resist the temptation to fall back into old patterns. As you walk away from this old pattern, ask Holy Spirit to rise in you and hold you accountable. Ask Him to help you build an *authentic* prayer life.

Matthew 21:13a CJB: *"He said to them, It has been written, __my house__ will be called a house of prayer."*

After Jesus kicked the money-changers out of the temple, he declared that **HIS HOUSE WILL BE CALLED** a house of prayer. Today, **you are His house** and he wants it clean so that He can dwell there. A ministry built on anything other than prayer is nothing more than a beautiful sandcastle resting on the bank of an ocean.

In truth, there is __nothing__ more important in your journey. To truly be like Christ is to engage in the most critical ministry on earth – that of intercession. Period. You will quickly begin getting correction, warnings, sound wisdom, counsel, guidance, revelation, strategy and understanding as you are pulled deeper into the bosom of Christ.

There is NO MINISTRY without the foundation of prayer.

Pray this prayer with me.

Father, in the name of your son Jesus Christ, I confess the sin of false evangelism. I confess that I have not represented you before your people in the way you commanded. I ask for forgiveness. I give Holy Spirit permission to lead and guide me in truth – uprooting every seed of entertainment, compromise, competition and comparison from my life. Father, uproot and sever every ungodly relationship, alignment, vow and agreement that I have made. I renounce the spiritual prostitution of my gifting and talents. I renounce spiritual adultery. I confess the sin of people pleasing and of wanting recognition, worship and acceptance from men. I renounce selfishness and greed, and my alliance with the world system. I renounce my pursuit of the wide gate – and every door that it has opened to me. Sever my relationship with this world and align me completely with your Kingdom. Cause me to take on your character, your philosophies and belief system in Jesus Name.

Holy Spirit, I give you permission to uproot any and all false teachings and false beliefs that have taken root in my soul and in my spirit. Fill those places with the truth of your Word. Holy Spirit, go before me and stand beside me ensuring that I do not return to these places of compromise in my life. Strengthen me dear Father in your will. I repent for knowing or unknowingly leading others outside of your will and I ask you to restore them quickly into their rightful places in you.

Teach me to follow the narrow gate according to your Word and to walk that path. Teach me to recognize the doors that you have opened to preach the Gospel and to embrace them boldly. I ask you Father to remove any hindrances that block my destiny and create in me a clean heart.

Give me, O Lord, a hunger and thirst for you, your presence, prayer and your Word. Open my ears that I may recognize and hear your voice.

I confess before Heaven and earth that I do not want to go anywhere unless your presence is with me. I confess that I don't want to do anything unless your presence is with me. Let my pursuit be for righteousness in Jesus Name. Close the doors in my life that you did not open. Stretch open the doors that you have designated for me in their appropriate timing and season.

Father, I repent for taking ownership over the gifts you've placed in me and over my life and ministry. I confess that I have been bought with a price by Jesus and that I am covered by His Blood. Today, Father I commit the work of my hands and all of me over to you. Use me Lord. I pray that I come forth in this season in the name of the BOOK that you have written for me. I pray that the thoughts and plans that you have for me – to give me a hope and a future – arise in me. I pray that I am a sheep who hears your voice and who will not follow the voice of a stranger.

Father, lead me into authentic relationships that you have designated for me and for my ministry. Lead me to those you have designated to help me stand in power, strength and authority in you. Lead me to those souls who are assigned to the ministry you've placed on the inside of me --- that they may receive all that you have for them. Equip me to lead and to move according to Isaiah 61. Father, hide me in the secret place, causing me to walk fully in the original intent and purposes for which you sent my soul from Heaven to earth in Jesus Name.

About Voices of Christ

For the past decade, Voices of Christ Literary Ministries International has served as a safe haven for Christian prophetic writers globally, specifically those who write the secret things the Lord reveals to their heart. By prophetic writers, we are referring to those who are Prophetic Scribes, Scribal Apostles or Scribal Prophets who write on all three levels of the Scribal Anointing -- administrative, creative and instructional. Holy Spirit has created an environment within us in which these writers, who are often overlooked and misunderstood, are loved, accepted, affirmed, activated and encouraged in their individuality and uniqueness in Jesus Christ.

We have become a place of refuge, safety and security for these writers where they uncover their identities through the word, walk out God's original purpose and intent for their scribal ministries, and take their rightful place in the Kingdom. Our membership includes poets, spoken word artists, playwrights, songwriters, children's book authors, journalists, novelists, devotionalists and writers of administration and instruction -- all operating under the **Matthew 13:52** anointing for the present day scribe. Our mission, vision and purpose are carried out through our prophetic School of the Scribe. We are not a performance or theatrical ministry -- however, we do walk out our divine creativity and ministry unto the Lord without inhibitions; and with passion and fervency for *souls*. We go into places where hope is needed like nursing homes, groups homes, community centers or wherever the Lord may need us to shine His light. But our mandate is ensuring that the scribes of the King are rooted in the word, making full proof of their ministries. Like the scribes of old, we believe in apprenticeship, and the "maturing" of the gift as the sons of God grow in their faith. Our prayer is that VOC will become a resource and home for you along your scribal journey, and that the peace and blessings of the Lord and *The Scribal Anointing* overtake you in this season.

Web: voicesofchrist.org

Social: scribalanointing.ning.com
facebook.com/voicesofchrist
twitter.com/voicesofchrist

Email: information@voicesofchrist.org